BEAUTIFUL BIRDS
COLORING BOOK

Dot Barlowe

DOVER PUBLICATIONS, INC.
MINEOLA, NEW YORK

This enchanting coloring collection features beautiful birds from all over the world. From the cardinal and the bluebird, to the ruby-throated hummingbird and the roseate spoonbill, each image has been meticulously rendered by wildlife artist Dot Barlowe. Each bird is featured in its natural habitat, and a detailed color guide can be found on the inside back cover. The latest edition to Dover's *Creative Haven* series for the experienced colorist, unbacked plates allow you to use any media you like, and the perforated pages make displaying your finished work easy.

Bibliographical Note

Beautiful Birds Coloring Book, first published by Dover Publications, Inc., in 2015, contains a selection of plates from the following previously published Dover books by Dot Barlowe: *Birds to Paint or Color* (2007), *America the Beautiful to Paint or Color* (2006), *Tropical Paradise Scenes to Paint or Color* (2009), and *Nautical Scenes to Paint or Color* (2007).

International Standard Book Number

ISBN-13: 978-0-486-80401-9
ISBN-10: 0-486-80401-1

Manufactured in the United States by RR Donnelley
80401108   2016
www.doverpublications.com

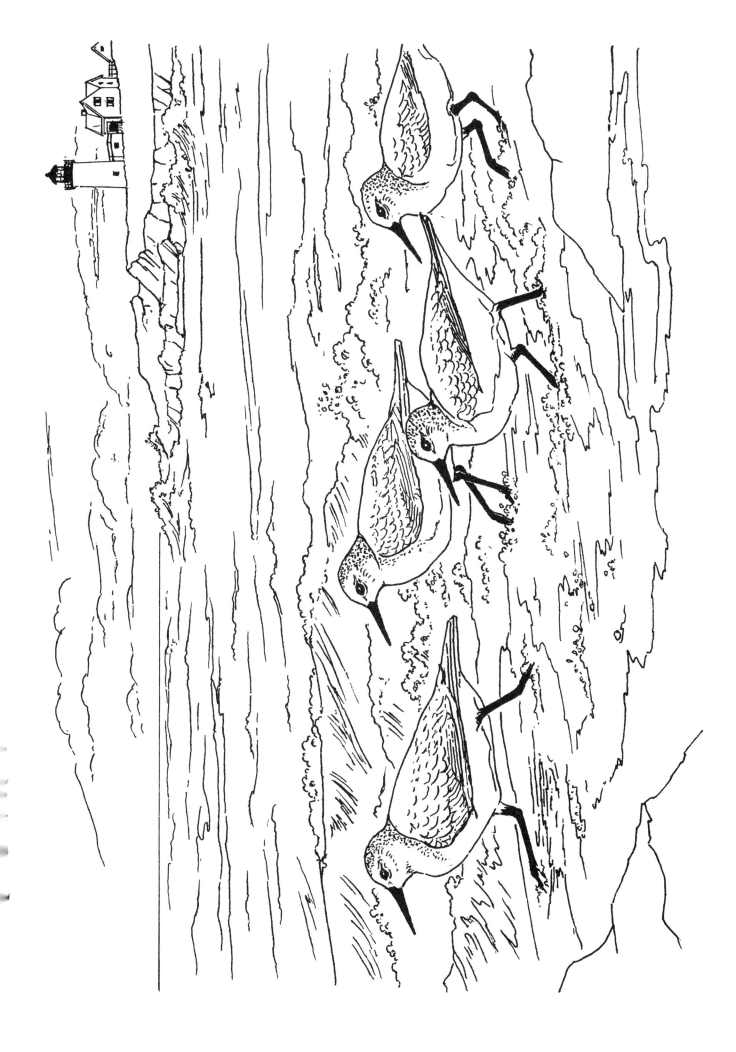